STUPENDOUS AND TREMENDOUS SCIENCE

ECSTATIC (AND EXCELLENT) ENERGY

ENTER A WORLD OF PETRIFYING POWER!

CLAUDIA MARTIN

Gareth Stevens PUBLISHING

Please visit our website,
www.garethstevens.com.
For a free color catalog of all
our high-quality books, call
toll free 1-800-542-2595 or
fax 1-877-542-2596.

Cataloging-in-Publication Data

Names: Martin, Claudia.
Title: Ecstatic (and excellent) energy / Claudia Martin.
Description: Buffalo, NY : Gareth Stevens Publishing, 2025. |
Series: Stupendous and tremendous science | Includes glossary
and index.
Identifiers: ISBN 9781482468755 (pbk.) |
ISBN 9781482468762 (library bound) | ISBN 9781482468779 (ebook)
Subjects: LCSH: Power resources--Juvenile literature.
Classification: LCC TJ163.23 M37 2025 | DDC 621.042--dc23

Published in 2025 by
Gareth Stevens Publishing
2544 Clinton St.
Buffalo, NY 14224

First published in Great Britain in 2022 by Wayland

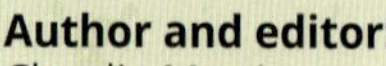

Author and editor:
Claudia Martin

Series designer:
Rocket Design (East Anglia) Ltd

Illustrator:
Steve Evans

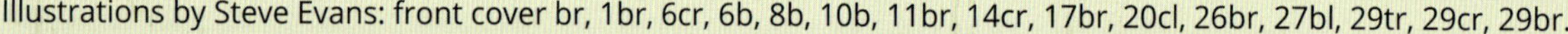

Illustrations by Steve Evans: front cover br, 1br, 6cr, 6b, 8b, 10b, 11br, 14cr, 17br, 20cl, 26br, 27bl, 29tr, 29cr, 29br.

Picture acknowledgements: iStock: NickyLloyd 5tr, fotosipsak 5cr, Svetlana Urbanskaya 9tl, Serg Velusceac 9tc; NASA/Solar Dynamics Observatory: 7b; Shutterstock: petovarga front cover l, 1bl, 30br, YummyBuum front cover bl, Vectorfair.com front cover tr, back cover, maglyvi 2cr, 9br, NotionPic 2c, 9bc, 11cr, lenoleum 4cl, Ratana Prongjai 5tl, Amit Avrahami 5cl, BonNontawat 5bcl, ssuaphotos 5bcl, vinap 5bl, Realchemyst 5bc, Petair 5br, VectorMine 7c, 20br, BlueRingMedia 9tr, Vector Plotnikoff 10–11, Pretty Vectors 12b, Narcissa Less 13cl, nafanya241 13b, shockfactor.de 13br, Onevector 14br, Inna Bigun 15tr, HIRO-Lab 15bl, Achiichiii 15br, VK1971 16tl, Jacek Chabraszewski 16tr, stewart beattie 16cl, insta_photos 16cr, Helioscribe 16br, Don Purcell 17tr, GraphicsRF.com 18b, Sergey Ryzhov 19tr, XiXinXing 19cr, Jenson 21tl, Okcamera 21tr, tackune 21cl, Funny Solution Studio 21cr, NIKS ADS 21bl, Gabi Wolf 22tr, 31tr, Alexander Knyazhinsky 22br, Drp8 23tr, Artur_Nyk 23bl, Vova Shevchuk 23bl, magnetix 24cr, YZm 24bl, engel.ac 25b, abriendomundo 26c, Bildagentur Zoonar GmbH 26cr, Breedfoto 27tl, Space-kraft 27tr, photostar72 27cl, naten 27cr.

All additional design elements from Shutterstock or drawn by designer.

Printed in the United States of America

CPSIA compliance information: Batch #CW25GS: For further information contact Gareth Stevens at 1-800-542-2595.

ECSTATIC AND EXCELLENT CONTENTS

ETERNAL ENERGY

Energy is all around you, from the electricity that makes a lightbulb glow to the food you eat so you can jump and dance. Without energy, there would be no movement, light, or life. Luckily for us, energy exists everywhere all of the time and can never run out!

WHAT IS ENERGY?

Energy is what gives everything and everyone the ability to do **work**. Work takes many forms, from running across the park to launching a space rocket. The energy for running comes from food, while a rocket's energy comes from its **fuel**. But everything contains energy. All things are made of tiny building blocks called **atoms**, too small to be seen by human eyes. Atoms are made of even smaller **particles** that are held together by forces that store energy. Atoms can also join together into groups called **molecules**, storing energy in the bonds between them.

IS ENERGY USEFUL?

Without energy, living things could not grow or live. Nothing could move or change. Energy cannot be created or destroyed, but it can change from one form to another. Humans have learned how to use this fact to their advantage. For example, the lightbulb was invented to change electrical energy into light and heat energy. We have also learned how to store energy – for example, in fuel or an electrical battery – then use it to do work when needed.

Many scientists say that all energy was created 13.8 billion years ago in the Big Bang, when the universe started to expand from a tiny point. Yet no one knows why the Big Bang happened!

ARE THERE DIFFERENT FORMS OF ENERGY?

The many different forms of energy can be divided into two main types: **kinetic energy** and **potential energy**. Kinetic energy is the energy of movement. Potential energy is stored energy, which can be used later. Here are some of the main forms of energy:

POTENTIAL ENERGY

CHEMICAL

ENERGY STORED IN FOOD AND FUEL

GRAVITATIONAL

ENERGY STORED IN ANYTHING THAT COULD FALL

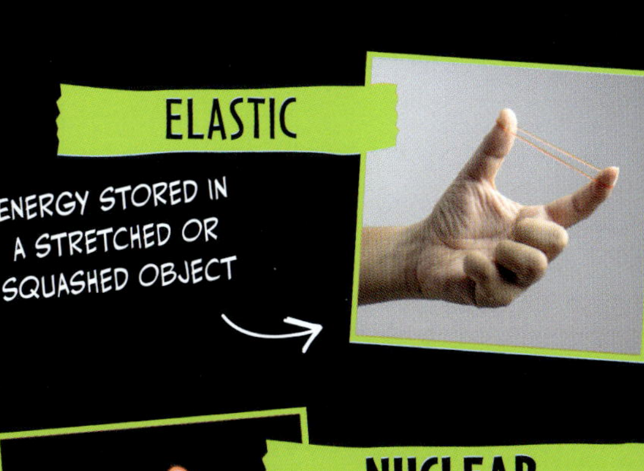

ELASTIC

ENERGY STORED IN A STRETCHED OR SQUASHED OBJECT

NUCLEAR

ENERGY STORED INSIDE ATOMS

KINETIC ENERGY

MECHANICAL

ENERGY OF OBJECTS IN MOTION

HEAT

ENERGY OF MOVING MOLECULES

LIGHT

ENERGY THAT TRAVELS IN WAVES

SOUND

ENERGY PRODUCED WHEN AN OBJECT VIBRATES

ELECTRICAL

ENERGY OF FLOWING, ELECTRICALLY CHARGED PARTICLES

WHAT A STAR!

The Sun is a star: a ball of hot gas. It reaches 27 million°F (15 million°C). Nearly all of Earth's energy comes from the Sun. We feel it as heat and see it as light. Without the Sun, there would be no plants, no animals – and no you!

WHERE DOES THE SUN'S ENERGY COME FROM?

Like everything else in the universe, the Sun cannot make energy. But it can release energy! More than 90 percent of the Sun's atoms are **hydrogen**. The Sun's core is so hot and tightly compacted that hydrogen atoms crash into each other. They join together to make a different type of atom, **helium** – and as they do so, they release energy.

HOW LONG DOES IT TAKE SUNLIGHT TO REACH EARTH?

It takes 8 minutes and 20 seconds for sunlight to travel the 93 million miles (149.6 million km) from the Sun to Earth. Light travels as waves, moving like the rising and falling of waves on the ocean. However, these waves are not water: they contain tiny, weightless, invisible bundles of energy, called **photons**.

DOES THE SUN JUST GIVE OFF LIGHT AND HEAT?

The energy radiated (given off) by the Sun is known as electromagnetic radiation. As well as light and heat, electromagnetic radiation has other forms. Each of these forms has different **wavelengths**, which are the distances between the top of one wave and the next. The longest wavelengths are **radio waves**, **microwaves**, and **infrared**. We can feel infrared as heat. In the middle of the range is the visible light that we can see (see page 10). The shortest wavelengths are **ultraviolet**, X-rays and **gamma rays**. These are so high energy they can be damaging to humans, but most do not make it through the **atmosphere** to Earth's surface.

SCIENTISTS DIVIDE ELECTROMAGNETIC RADIATION INTO SEVEN TYPES:

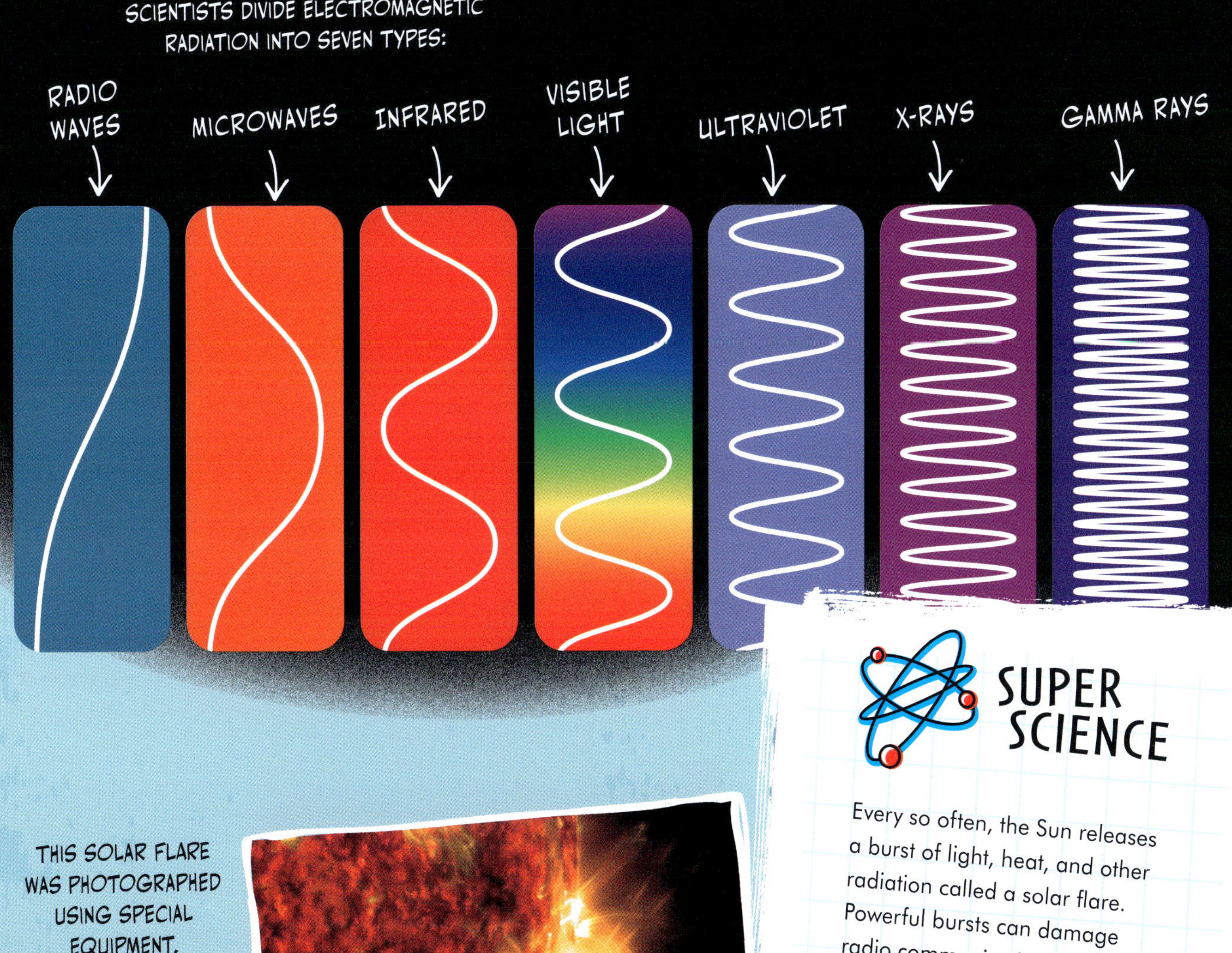

SUPER SCIENCE

Every so often, the Sun releases a burst of light, heat, and other radiation called a solar flare. Powerful bursts can damage radio communications and **electricity** supplies on Earth. Scientists try to predict solar flares by studying the Sun's behavior, which follows an 11-year pattern of high and low activity.

THIS SOLAR FLARE WAS PHOTOGRAPHED USING SPECIAL EQUIPMENT.

YOU SHOULD NEVER LOOK AT THE SUN DIRECTLY OR THROUGH A TELESCOPE OR CAMERA, AS ITS BRIGHTNESS WILL DAMAGE YOUR EYES.

FEELING HOT!

Everything around you has heat energy, including the book you are reading. Heat energy is created by the movement of an object's atoms and molecules. These are always in motion: shaking, bumping, or darting!

HOW COLD CAN THINGS GET?

The hotter an object gets, the more its molecules move. In a solid, such as ice, the molecules are packed tightly. They can only vibrate. If more heat energy is added, the molecules gain enough energy to break apart from each other, melting ice into liquid water. Now the molecules can slide around. If even more heat is added, water becomes a gas called water vapor. In a gas, the molecules dart around fast and freely.

There is a temperature at which all the molecules in an object are still and it can get no colder. Called absolute zero, this temperature is -459.67°F (-273.15°C).

FACT

We often measure temperature using the Fahrenheit or Celsius scales. The Celsius scale was developed by Anders Celsius in 1742. Today, the temperature at which ice melts is set at 0°C, with 100°C as the temperature at which water boils. However, in Celsius's original scale, the values were reversed: the boiling point was 0°C and freezing was 100°C.

WHY DOES GLASS FEEL COLD?

Heat energy always moves from something hot to something colder. There are three ways that heat energy transfers: conduction, radiation, and convection.

CONDUCTION

CONDUCTION TRANSFERS HEAT ENERGY BETWEEN OR THROUGH OBJECTS, AS SOME ENERGY OF A HOT PARTICLE TRANSFERS TO ANY COOLER PARTICLES IT TOUCHES. WHEN YOU TOUCH GLASS, SOME HEAT FROM YOUR HAND IS TRANSFERRED TO THE COLDER GLASS, MAKING YOUR HAND FEEL COOLER.

RADIATION

RADIATION TRANSFERS HEAT ENERGY AS INFRARED WAVES (SEE PAGE 7). HEAT WAVES SPREAD OUTWARD FROM ANY HOT OBJECT. WHEN THE WAVES REACH ANOTHER OBJECT, THEY WARM IT.

CONVECTION

CONVECTION TRANSFERS HEAT THROUGH GASES AND LIQUIDS. WHEN WATER IS HEATED IN A PAN, THE WATER AT THE BOTTOM HEATS UP FIRST, MAKING IT RISE. COLDER WATER THEN FLOWS TO THE BOTTOM, CREATING A CIRCULAR MOVEMENT UNTIL ALL THE WATER IS THE SAME TEMPERATURE.

WHY DOESN'T A POLAR BEAR SHIVER?

Polar bears are not cold in their Arctic habitat because they are well insulated. Insulation slows down the transfer of heat between something warm (the polar bear) and something cool (its surroundings). Both trapped air and fat are good insulators, as heat does not travel easily through them by conduction. A polar bear has a layer of fat as well as thick fur that traps lots of air.

LOVELY LIGHT

During the day, we get light from the hot Sun. At night, we get it from the hot wires inside lightbulbs. Light is made of photons, which are given off by atoms when they get hot.

WHAT MAKES A RAINBOW?

Although sunlight looks white, it is made up of all the colors of the rainbow, called the spectrum. Each of these colors of light has a slightly different wavelength (see page 7). When sunlight shines through water droplets in the air during a rain shower, we can see all the colors in a rainbow. This is because the raindrops bend and separate the light waves.

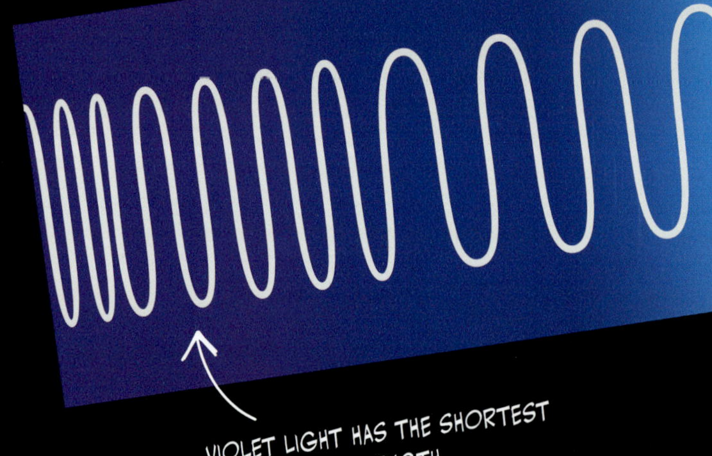

VIOLET LIGHT HAS THE SHORTEST WAVELENGTH.

WHY DOES AN ORANGE LOOK ... ORANGE?

We see things because light bounces off them into our eyes. We see objects as different colors because of how they reflect or **absorb** light. Our eyes see only the colors that are reflected. We see an object as black if it absorbs all colors. An object looks white if it reflects every color. An orange looks orange because it reflects orange light and absorbs the rest of the spectrum.

SUPER SCIENCE

Some animals make their own light using chemicals called luciferins that release energy. This is called bioluminescence. These animals, such as fireflies, use light to attract prey or mates in the dark. Doctors are experimenting with luciferins to fight cancer. Cancer causes cells to multiply in ways that harm the body. By injecting cancer cells with luciferins and a chemical that makes them sensitive to light, doctors can make the cells self-destruct.

WHY DO YOUR LEGS LOOK WOBBLY IN A SWIMMING POOL?

Light cannot travel through most materials, which is why many things cast a shadow. However, light can travel through transparent materials, such as water or glass. When light travels from air into water, it is bent. This bending is called refraction. It is caused by light not being able to travel as fast through water as it can through air. It means that, when looked at from a certain angle, your legs appear to bend when you are in a swimming pool!

HMMM. STRANGE ...

SHAKY, SHAKY SOUND

Sound energy is produced when we make an object vibrate. That shaking object might be a cymbal or the vocal cords we use to speak. The sound energy travels in all directions as waves, called sound waves!

WHAT MAKES YOUR EAR DRUM QUIVER?

When we crash a cymbal, the cymbal shakes. This makes the surrounding air molecules vibrate, which makes all the molecules they are touching vibrate, too. The **vibration** travels through the air in the form of a wave. Each molecule passes on a little less energy than it received, which is why sounds get quieter the farther away you are from their source. When a sound wave reaches your ears, it travels down the ear canal to the eardrum. This skin is thin and stretched tight like a drum, so sound waves make it vibrate.

FREAKY FACT

Sound energy travels much slower than light energy, which is why we hear thunder after we see the lightning that has made the noise. Sound travels at speeds of 767 miles (1,235 km) per hour, but light travels at 670,616,629 miles (1,079,252,849 km) per hour.

WHAT HAPPENS INSIDE YOUR EAR?

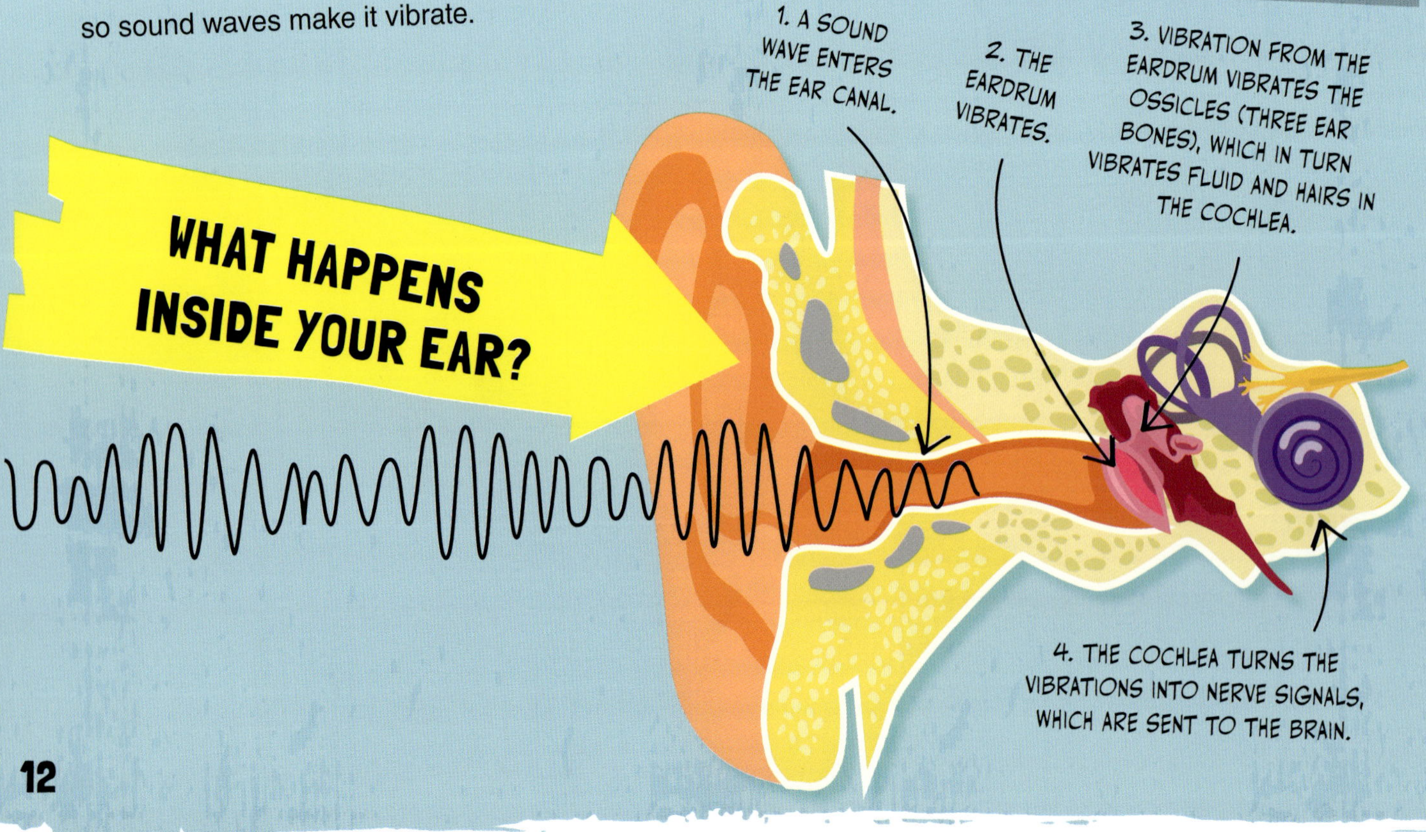

WHY DOES A VIOLIN SOUND DIFFERENT FROM A FLUTE?

Sounds have different pitches, which is how low or high they are. When an object's sound waves vibrate fast, we hear the sound as a high pitch. When the vibrations are slower, we hear a lower pitch. The faster the vibration, the less time there is between each wave. Musical instruments are made of different materials and are played differently, such as by plucking a string or blowing air through a tube. This gives instruments different pitches (wavelengths) and qualities (wave shapes).

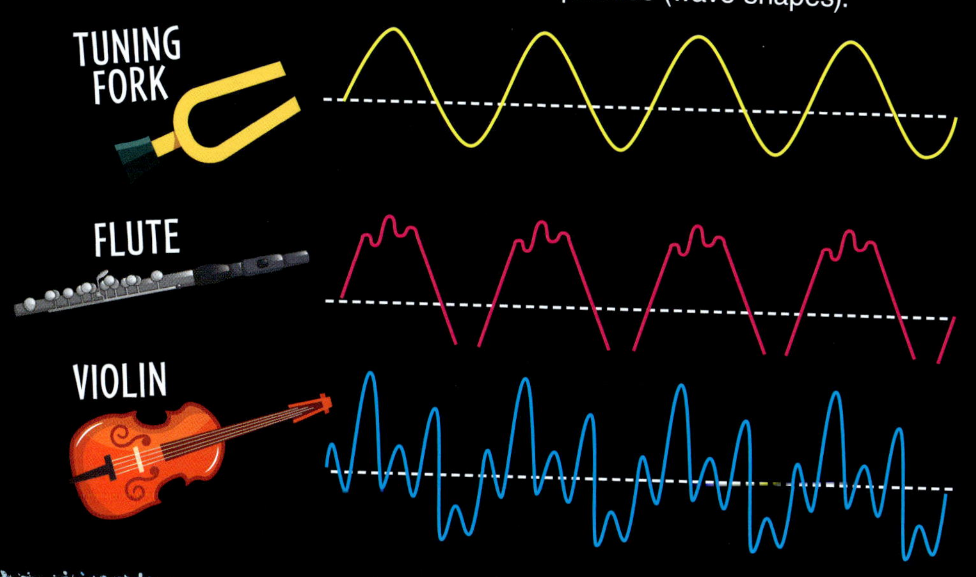

THESE SOUND WAVES SHOW A TUNING FORK, VIOLIN, AND FLUTE PLAYING A NOTE WITH THE SAME PITCH, SO THERE IS EQUAL TIME BETWEEN THEIR WAVES. WHILE THE TUNING FORK MAKES A PURE NOTE, THE FLUTE AND VIOLIN MAKE COMPLEX SOUNDS, SO THEIR WAVE SHAPES ARE DIFFERENT.

WHY DO YODELERS LOVE MOUNTAINS?

When we speak, sing, or yodel, we are making sounds by vibrating our vocal cords. These are folds of tissue in the throat. We make them vibrate by breathing air out of our lungs and through the cords. In the Alps (a mountain range in Europe), people developed a dramatic style of yodeling – a high-pitched tuneful yelling – to call their cows and to pass on messages. Sound waves can bounce off hard surfaces, creating an echo. In the Alps, a yodeler's yelling bounces off surrounding mountains, so the sound is heard again and again.

CRUCIAL CHEMICAL ENERGY

Chemical energy is essential for all life on our planet. This stored energy is found in the bonds that connect the atoms to atoms and molecules to molecules in a substance. Chemical energy is found in fabulously useful food and fuel.

WHY ARE PLANTS IMPORTANT?

On Earth, the Sun is our main source of energy. Yet animals have no way of turning sunlight into energy that they can use for growing and working. However, some animals can get energy from eating plants. Plants soak up sunlight using a green chemical called chlorophyll. Using this energy, plants change carbon dioxide gas from the air and water from the soil into sugar, which contains chemical energy. This amazing process is called photosynthesis. This stored (or potential) energy is used by plants for growing. When a plant is eaten by a plant-eating animal, some of the energy is passed on. Energy is then passed on along the food chain to meat-eating animals that eat the plant-eaters!

HOW DOES FOOD GIVE US ENERGY?

Chemical energy is potential energy (see page 5) that can be released by a **chemical reaction**. In a chemical reaction, the molecules of two or more substances separate then recombine to create new substances. In the human body, a series of chemical reactions breaks down food and releases energy that our **cells** use, so we can grow, work, and stay warm. This process starts in the mouth, continues in the stomach and intestines, and finishes in the body's trillions of cells.

MARVELOUS MOUTH

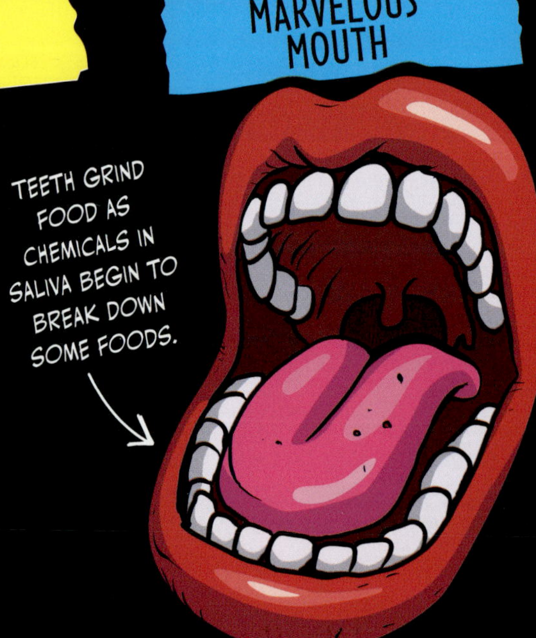

WHY IS FIRE HOT?

Something that can be burned to produce heat is called a fuel. When a fuel – such as wood, coal, or oil – gets very hot, it burns. This is a chemical reaction called combustion. Combustion turns fuel and oxygen (from the air) into the gases carbon dioxide and water vapor. The reaction also releases lots of energy as heat and light.

COMBUSTION IS A USEFUL REACTION BECAUSE THE ENERGY RELEASED CAN COOK FOOD, HEAT WATER, AND KEEP US WARM. IT IS ALSO A VERY DANGEROUS REACTION AS FIRE SPREADS FAST AND CAN KILL.

FACT

The human body's fat cells store any extra chemical energy for use later. A healthy adult's 30 billion fat cells store enough energy to power their body for several weeks.

SUPER STOMACH AND INTESTINES

CHEMICALS IN THE STOMACH AND INTESTINES BREAK FOOD INTO SIMPLE MOLECULES, WHICH ARE SOAKED UP THROUGH THE INTESTINE WALLS INTO THE BLOOD.

SCINTILLATING CELLS

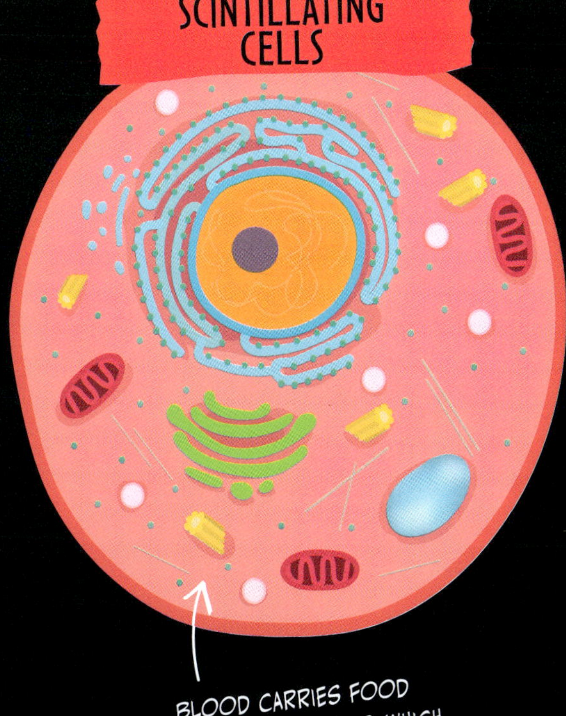

BLOOD CARRIES FOOD MOLECULES TO CELLS, WHICH CARRY OUT REACTIONS TO RELEASE ENERGY.

MOVING ALONG ...

Every object or animal that moves is using mechanical energy. We see mechanical energy at work when we watch flying birds, speeding cars, and running kids.

WHERE DOES MECHANICAL ENERGY COME FROM?

Mechanical energy is a form of kinetic (or movement) energy. Like all forms of energy, mechanical energy cannot be made; it can only be converted from other forms of energy. Here are some common examples of mechanical energy and where they come from:

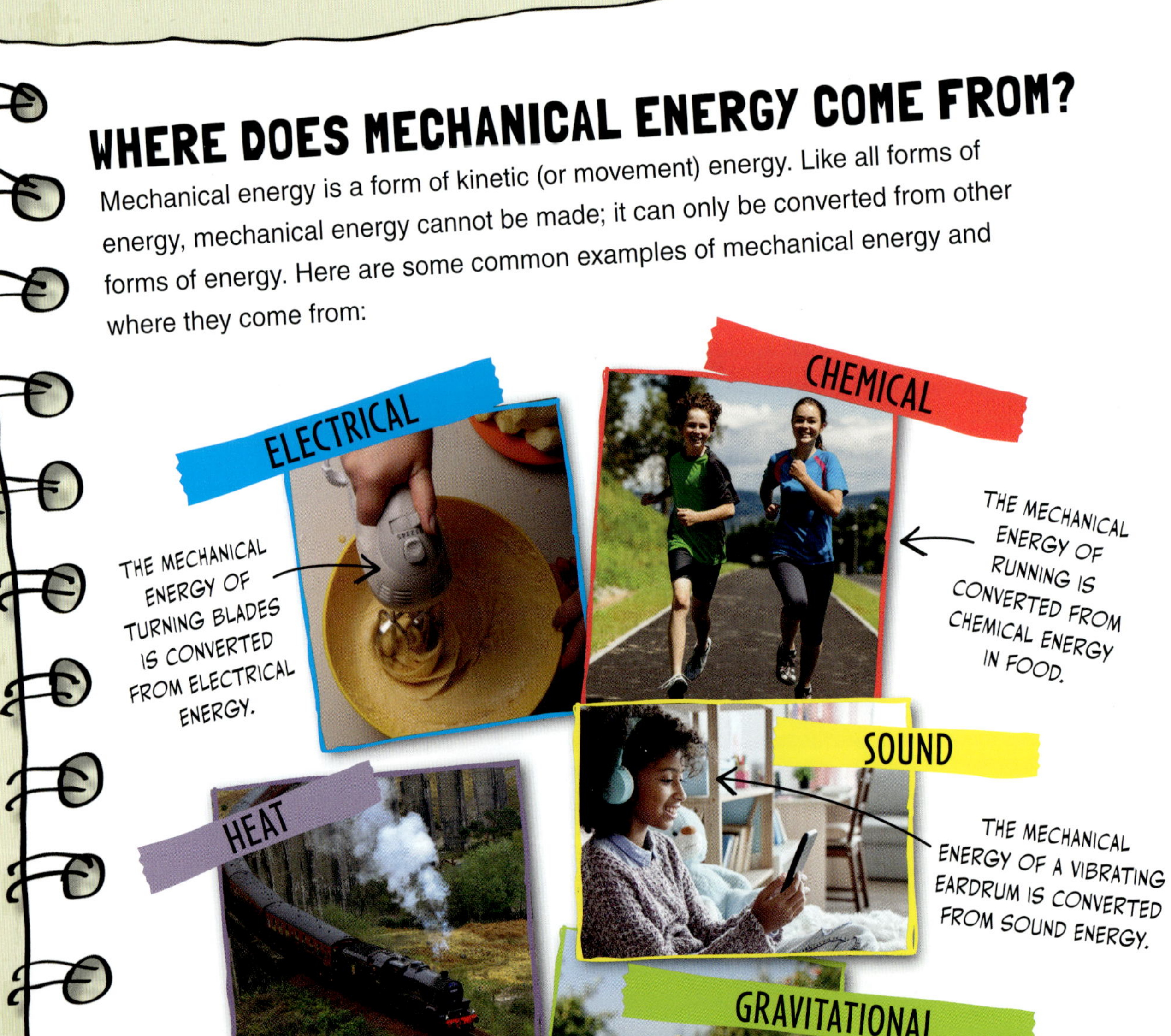

THE MECHANICAL ENERGY OF TURNING BLADES IS CONVERTED FROM ELECTRICAL ENERGY.

THE MECHANICAL ENERGY OF RUNNING IS CONVERTED FROM CHEMICAL ENERGY IN FOOD.

THE MECHANICAL ENERGY OF A VIBRATING EARDRUM IS CONVERTED FROM SOUND ENERGY.

THE MECHANICAL ENERGY OF A MOVING STEAM TRAIN IS CONVERTED FROM HEAT ENERGY.

THE MECHANICAL ENERGY OF A FALLING APPLE IS CONVERTED FROM GRAVITATIONAL ENERGY (SEE PAGE 18).

HOW DO BOWLING BALLS KNOCK DOWN PINS?

Mechanical energy can be passed on. This is what happens when a bowling ball hits pins. Since the ball is heavier than the pins, the ball's energy is enough to send the pins flying! Mechanical energy is transferred in lots of other very useful situations, like when a hammer drives a nail into a wall or when you swing a tennis racket to send a ball over the net.

WHY DO BICYCLE BRAKES GET HOT?

Since energy can never be destroyed, when you bring a bicycle to a stop by squeezing the brakes, something has to happen to the bicycle's mechanical energy. As the brakes press on the wheels, the brakes get hot. This is caused by friction, a force that always works in the opposite direction to the direction in which an object is moving. Friction converts much of the bicycle's mechanical energy to heat energy. You may also hear squealing from the brakes, as some energy is converted to sound energy.

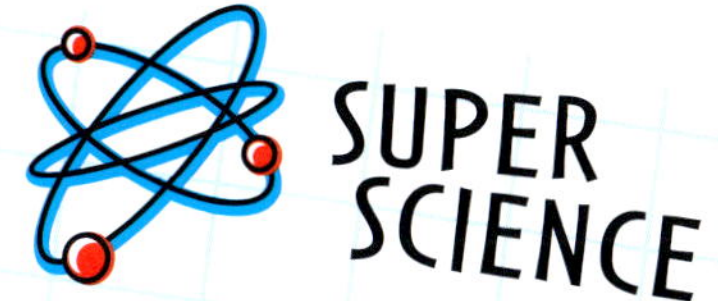

SUPER SCIENCE

Until the 1990s, scientists thought they knew about all the forms of energy that exist. Then they noticed that something was making the universe expand faster and faster. They wondered if it might be a mysterious force they called "dark energy." We cannot see the effects of dark energy on Earth, only in the way it seems to pull vast galaxies.

LOTS OF POTENTIAL

Potential energy is energy that has the potential – or possibility – to do work. For example, an object has potential energy if it is high – because it could fall! An object also has potential energy if it is stretched – because it could snap!

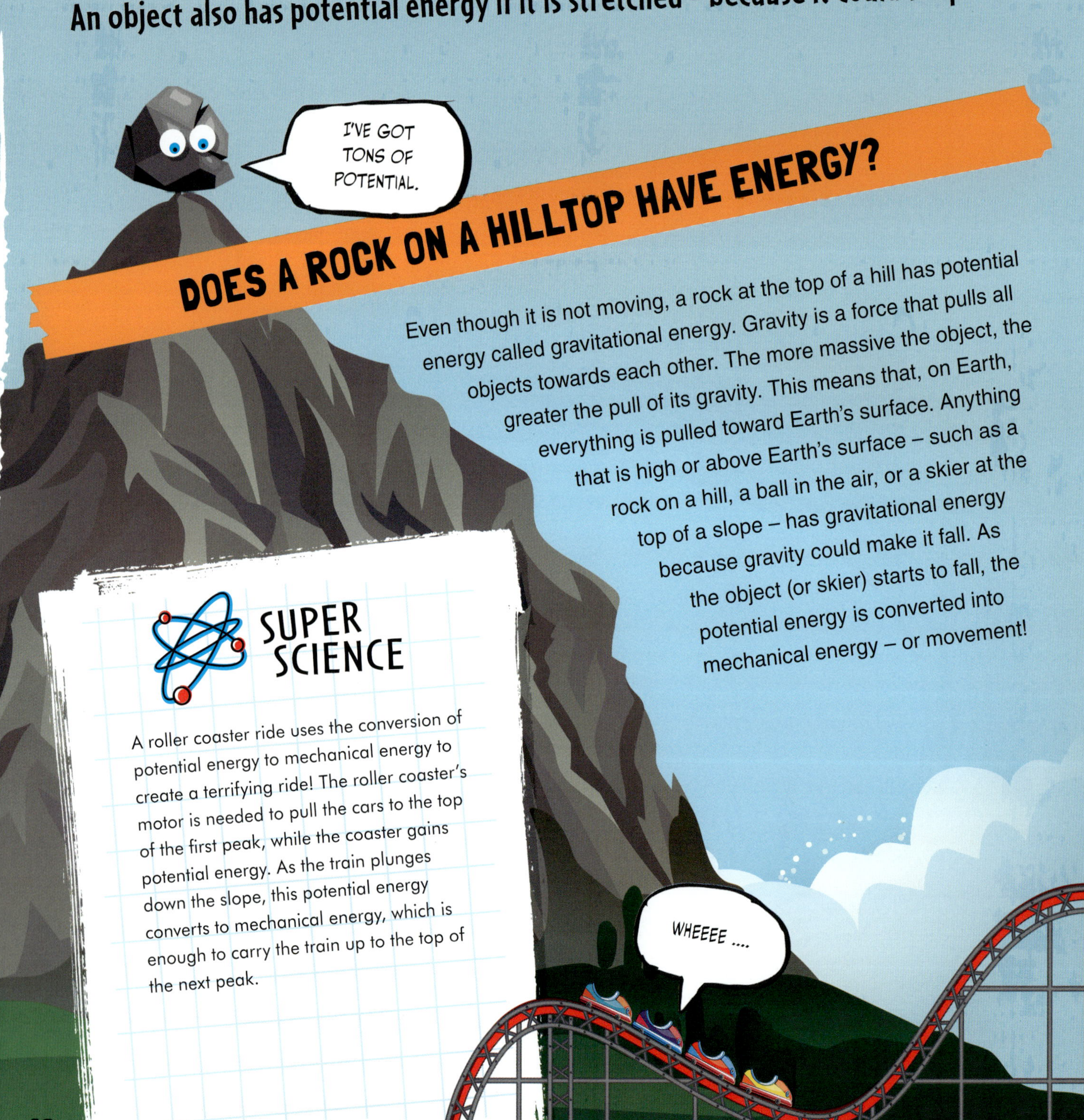

DOES A ROCK ON A HILLTOP HAVE ENERGY?

Even though it is not moving, a rock at the top of a hill has potential energy called gravitational energy. Gravity is a force that pulls all objects towards each other. The more massive the object, the greater the pull of its gravity. This means that, on Earth, everything is pulled toward Earth's surface. Anything that is high or above Earth's surface – such as a rock on a hill, a ball in the air, or a skier at the top of a slope – has gravitational energy because gravity could make it fall. As the object (or skier) starts to fall, the potential energy is converted into mechanical energy – or movement!

SUPER SCIENCE

A roller coaster ride uses the conversion of potential energy to mechanical energy to create a terrifying ride! The roller coaster's motor is needed to pull the cars to the top of the first peak, while the coaster gains potential energy. As the train plunges down the slope, this potential energy converts to mechanical energy, which is enough to carry the train up to the top of the next peak.

HOW DOES AN ARROW FIRE FROM A BOW?

Elastic potential energy is the energy that an elastic object has if it is stretched or squeezed. That elastic object might be an elastic band, a spring, a squeezy ball, or the string in a bow. The elastic energy is stored until the force used to stretch or squeeze the object is removed. In the case of the bow, that force is provided by the archer's hand and arm. When released, the elastic object springs back to its original shape, doing work in the process. In the case of a bow, this work is launching an arrow through the air.

THE WORK DONE BY THIS STRETCHED STRING WILL LAUNCH AN ARROW!

SQUEEZE!

THE WORK DONE BY THIS SQUEEZED SPRING WILL BOUNCE THE POGO-ER INTO THE AIR!

WHY DON'T BALLS BOUNCE FOREVER?

When you drop a ball, its gravitational energy becomes mechanical energy as it falls. Balls are made of an elastic material or filled with air, so when they hit the ground they are squashed, creating elastic potential energy. As the ball returns to its original shape, it springs back up. However, some of the ball's energy is lost as heat and sound energy during the collision with the ground. This means the ball bounces up with a little less energy than it bounced downward. With each bounce, the ball loses a little more energy and a little more height until it stops.

EXCITING ELECTRICITY

Electricity provides most of the energy that is needed by homes, schools, factories, and offices. Electricity flows down wires or is released from batteries, then powers machines – from computers to cars.

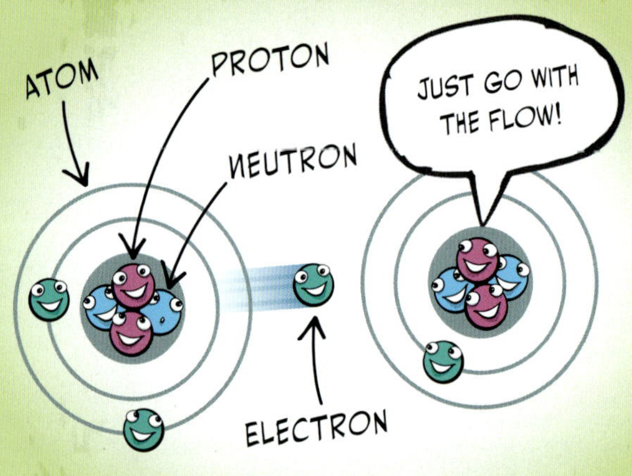

WHEN ELECTRICITY FLOWS THROUGH A WIRE, ELECTRONS ARE BEING BUMPED FROM ONE ATOM TO THE NEXT.

WHAT IS ELECTRICITY?

Atoms have tiny particles, called **electrons**, swirling around their center, called the **nucleus**. The nucleus is made of **protons** and **neutrons**. Electrons carry a negative electric charge, protons carry a positive charge, and neutrons have no charge. Opposite charges attract, but similar charges **repel**. Electrons push each other away! When electrons are pushed from atom to atom, the result is an electric current. Electrons move easily between atoms in metals such as copper, so electrical wires are often made of copper.

HOW DO MAGNETS MAKE ELECTRICITY?

At power plants, electricity is made by machines called **generators**. Generators create an electric current by moving a magnet past a coil of wire. This pushes electrons through the wire, which carries the electric current where it is needed. Batteries create electricity in a different way: In a battery, energy is stored in chemicals. When the battery is used in a machine, the chemical energy is converted into electrical energy.

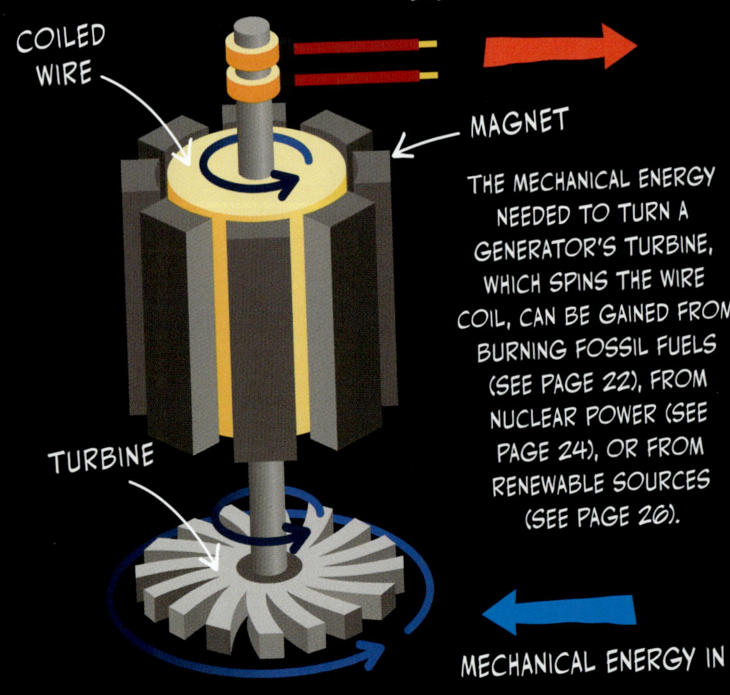

THE MECHANICAL ENERGY NEEDED TO TURN A GENERATOR'S TURBINE, WHICH SPINS THE WIRE COIL, CAN BE GAINED FROM BURNING FOSSIL FUELS (SEE PAGE 22), FROM NUCLEAR POWER (SEE PAGE 24), OR FROM RENEWABLE SOURCES (SEE PAGE 26).

HOW MUCH ELECTRICITY DO HUMANS USE?

Every year, humankind uses more than 22 trillion **kilowatt-hours** of electricity. A kilowatt-hour is a unit of energy equal to 1 kilowatt of power sustained for 1 hour. A small electric heater uses around 1 kilowatt. It takes more than 60,000 power plants to supply the world's electricity. Here are some of the main uses of electricity:

MANUFACTURING

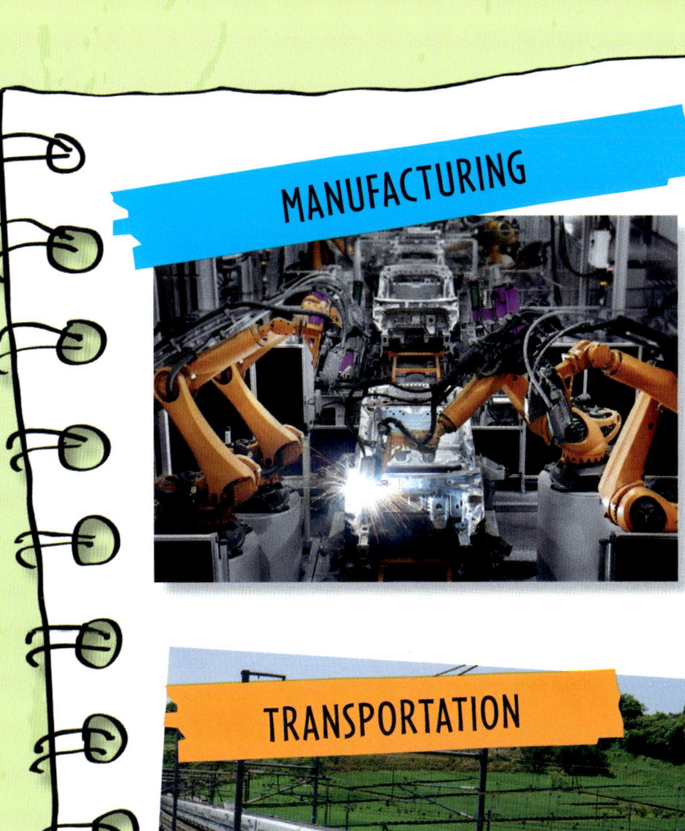

HEATING

TRANSPORTATION

LIGHTING

COMMUNICATION

FREAKY FACT

Electric eels are fish that make electricity in special body parts to stun predators and prey. They release electric shocks of up to 0.5 kilowatt-hours, which is enough to stun animals as big as horses.

FREAKY FOSSIL FUELS

Coal, oil, and natural gas are called fossil fuels. When these fuels are burned, they release heat. We use this energy to generate electricity, power factories, run cars, and cook food. We use a huge amount of fossil fuels – too much, in fact!

HOW DID FOSSIL FUELS GET THEIR ENERGY?

Millions of years ago, fossil fuels were plants and animals! The plants stored chemical energy they converted from light energy, while the animals stored energy from food (see page 14). When the plants and animals died, they were buried by mud. Over millions of years, they were pressed and heated underground until they changed into coal, oil, and natural gas. Today, oil and gas can be pumped from the ground, while coal is dug from mines.

WHICH FUEL DO WE USE MOST?

As of 2022, around 80 percent of the energy used in businesses, homes, and transportation comes from fossil fuels. Coal and natural gas each provide around a quarter of the world's energy. The biggest users of coal are factories and power plants. In power plants, burning coal creates steam or another kind of gas, which flows to turn turbines (see page 20). Natural gas is also burned to make electricity, as well as to cook food and heat homes. The fuel we use most is oil, which provides around a third of the world's energy. Oil's most common use is powering vehicles from cars to airplanes.

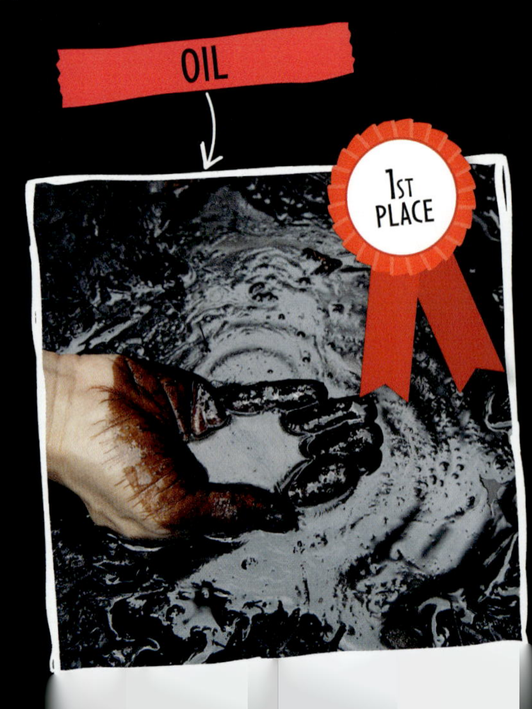

WHAT'S THE PROBLEM WITH FOSSIL FUELS?

One of the big problems with fossil fuels is that, when they are burned, they release gases such as carbon dioxide and methane. When these gases build up in the atmosphere in large quantities, they trap too much of the Sun's heat. Burning fossil fuels is heating Earth's air and oceans. Rising temperatures are causing more extreme weather and disasters, such as storms, floods, droughts, and wildfires.

SUN

HEAT AND LIGHT

ATMOSPHERE

EARTH

CARBON DIOXIDE IS KNOWN AS A GREENHOUSE GAS BECAUSE, BY WARMING EARTH, IT ACTS A LITTLE LIKE THE GLASS OF A GREENHOUSE.

FREAKY FACT

Earth's average surface temperature has risen by around 2°F (1°C) since the late 19th century, mostly because of burning fossil fuels and other human activities. Although this sounds like a small change, it has been enough to damage habitats and change weather patterns.

COAL

NATURAL GAS

GOING NUCLEAR

Around one-tenth of the world's electricity comes from nuclear energy. Across the world, there are about 440 nuclear power plants, all releasing huge amounts of energy from atoms too tiny to see!

WHAT IS NUCLEAR ENERGY?

Nuclear energy is the energy stored inside atoms by the forces that hold together the nucleus. By splitting a large atom into smaller atoms, a massive amount of energy can be released. This splitting is called nuclear fission. In nuclear power plants, the energy from atoms is released carefully to create heat. This boils water to make steam, which powers generators to make electricity (see page 20).

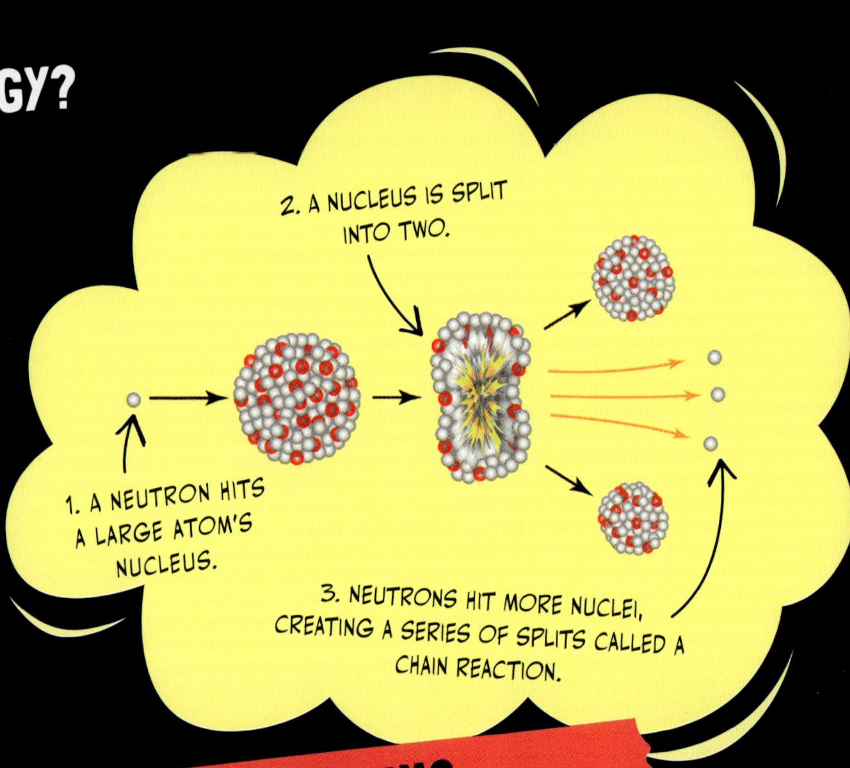

WHAT'S USEFUL ABOUT URANIUM?

Uranium was discovered in 1789 by German scientist Martin Heinrich Klaproth. Uranium is a metal that is made of large atoms. Most nuclear power plants use a particular type of uranium, called U-235, because its atoms are easy to split. Amazingly, 2.2 pounds (1 kg) of coal gives 8 kilowatt-hours of heat, but 2.2 pounds (1 kg) of U-235 gives 24,000,000 kilowatt-hours!

KLAPROTH NAMED URANIUM AFTER THE PLANET URANUS, WHICH HAD RECENTLY BEEN DISCOVERED. URANUS WAS THE GREEK GOD OF THE SKY.

IS NUCLEAR ENERGY DANGEROUS?

The energy of uncontrolled nuclear fission, which is released by nuclear bombs, can destroy cities. Yet in a power plant, chain reactions are slowed or stopped to keep everybody safe. Accidents are very rare, but they occasionally happen in old-fashioned power plants. In 2011, a Japanese nuclear power plant was damaged by an earthquake and **tsunami**, forcing people who lived nearby to abandon their homes. An everyday issue with nuclear power plants is that they produce **radioactive** waste, which gives off powerful energy that damages living things. Most countries have strict laws about getting rid of radioactive waste.

EXCESS HEAT ENERGY IS RELEASED SAFELY THROUGH THE GIANT COOLING TOWERS AT TIHANGE NUCLEAR POWER STATION IN BELGIUM. UNLIKE FOSSIL FUELS, NUCLEAR POWER DOES NOT RELEASE CARBON DIOXIDE AND WORSEN CLIMATE CHANGE.

SUPER SCIENCE

In modern nuclear power plants, a safety device called a core catcher is installed to surround and cool any hot, molten fuel if there was ever an accident. Core catchers are encased by superstrong concrete that do not easily conduct heat, crack, or burn.

REALLY RENEWABLE

If we continue to rely on fossil fuels, they may run out. Energy sources that will never run out are called renewable. In 2023, around one-third of the world's electricity came from renewable sources, but that fraction is growing ...

WHAT IS RENEWABLE ENERGY?

Renewable energy comes from resources that are made by natural processes, so they are constantly replenished. In contrast, although fossil fuels form naturally, they take millions of years to do it. Unlike fossil fuels, most renewable energy sources do not release carbon dioxide, so they do not worsen climate change.

SUPERB SOLAR

SOLAR PANELS CONVERT SUNLIGHT INTO ELECTRICITY.

Bountiful Biomass

PLANTS AND ANIMAL WASTE ARE MADE INTO FUEL FOR VEHICLES OR BURNED FOR HEAT OR ELECTRICITY GENERATION.

IS USING GEOTHERMAL ENERGY A NEW IDEA?

When Earth formed around 4.5 billion years ago, it was superhot. The planet has gone through many periods of cooling since then. However, in certain places inside Earth's crust (its outer layer), it is still so hot that water boils and rock melts. Hot springs are where geothermally heated groundwater, from rain or underground rivers, rises to the surface. For thousands of years, people have been using hot springs for washing, heating, and cooking.

THE ROMANS USED HOT SPRINGS TO HEAT PUBLIC BATHS.

FREAKY FACT

The International Space Station, which orbits 250 miles (400 km) above Earth, gets its electricity from solar panels. Solar panels hold trillions of silicon atoms, which release electrons (see page 20) when hit by sunlight.

Wonderful Wind

THE WIND'S MECHANICAL ENERGY TURNS WIND TURBINES.

Outstanding Ocean

TURBINES HARNESS THE MECHANICAL ENERGY OF TIDES.

HEAT INSIDE EARTH GENERATES ELECTRICITY AND WARMS WATER.

Gorgeous Geothermal

Helpful Hydroelectric

DAMMED WATER FALLS THROUGH TURBINES TO TURN ELECTRICITY GENERATORS.

HOW DO SEA SNAKES MAKE ELECTRICITY?

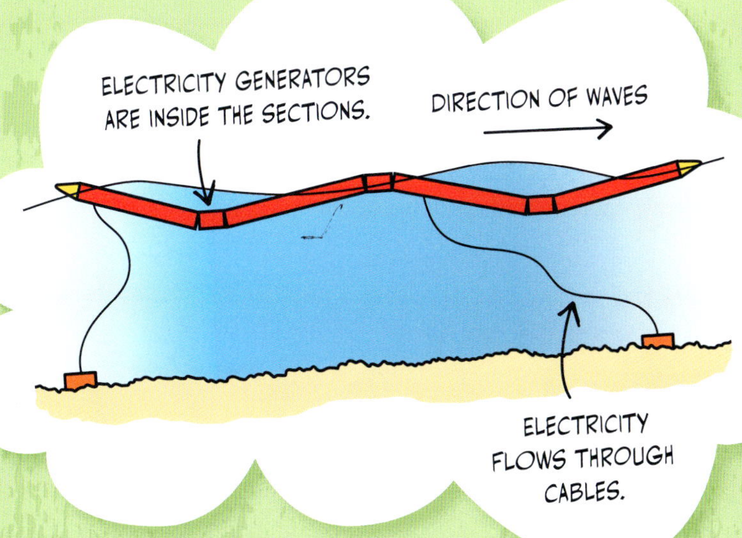

Machines nicknamed sea snakes have been used to generate electricity from ocean waves. Waves are made by wind blowing over the ocean's surface. Snake-like devices with many sections float on the water's surface at right angles to the direction of the waves. The waves make the sections move against each other. This mechanical energy drives electricity generators.

ASTONISHING ACTIVITY:

STATIC ELECTRICITY RACE

In this thrilling race, we will roll drink cans across the floor using only the power of **static electricity**! This is a form of electricity caused by a build-up of electrons in an object. It can be created by rubbing objects together.

YOU WILL NEED:

ONE EMPTY ALUMINUM DRINK CAN PER RACER (ASK AN ADULT TO CHECK FOR SHARP EDGES)

ONE BALLOON PER RACER

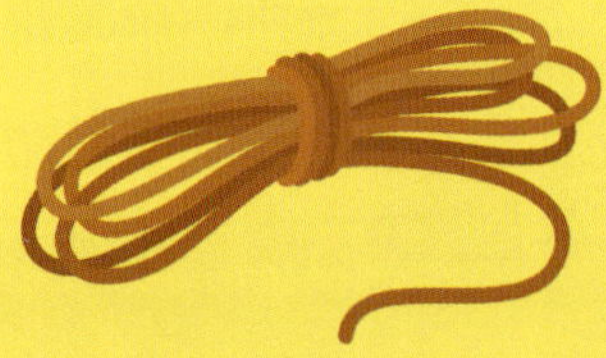

STRING

SCISSORS (ASK FOR AN ADULT'S HELP)

TAPE MEASURE

1. Make sure your can is clean and dry, as a wet can will not race. Choose a flat, smooth area of floor or ground that is at least 6 feet (2 m) long and 3 feet (1 m) wide.

2. Cut two pieces of string, each around 3 feet (1 m) long. These will be your start and finish lines, so if more than two people will be racing at once, you may need to make your strings longer.

3. Lay the starting line string flat and straight on the ground. Using your tape measure, lay the finish line string exactly parallel with the start line and 6 feet (2 m) away.

4 Ask an adult to help each racer blow up a balloon.

5 Each racer should charge their balloon by rubbing it back and forth on their hair really fast. What happens to each racer's hair?

6 Lay the cans on their sides along the start line. On a "1-2-3 … Go!" signal, each racer should place their balloon about 1 inch (2.5 cm) in front of their can, which will make the can roll toward it. Each racer needs to move their can along the course using their balloon.

7 If any racer's can touches their balloon or any part of their body, they must go back to the starting line!

8 The winner is the racer who gets their can across the finish line first!

COOL CONCLUSION

Static electricity is created by moving around tiny electric charges. Atoms usually contain an equal number of protons, with a positive electric charge, and electrons, with a negative charge (see page 20). Opposite charges attract, but similar charges repel. When you rubbed the balloon on your hair, you created static electricity by rubbing electrons off your hair onto the balloon. Now your hair had more protons than electrons, so it had a positive charge, while the balloon was negatively charged. Your hair was attracted to the balloon, so it stuck to it!

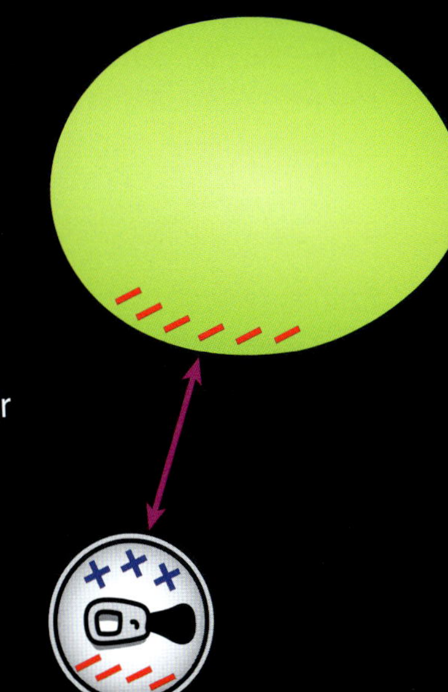

When the negatively charged balloon was held close to the can, the can's electrons moved to the other side of the can. In metals such as aluminium, electrons move easily. This gave a positive charge to the side of the can closest to the balloon. The attraction between the balloon's electrons and the can's protons made the can roll.

GLOSSARY

absorb to soak up

atmosphere the blanket of gases that surrounds Earth

atom the smallest part of any substance that can exist on its own

cell the tiniest building block of all living things

chemical energy energy that is stored in the bonds between atoms and molecules

chemical reaction a process in which one or more substances are converted into different substances, usually releasing chemical energy

electricity energy resulting from charged electons and protons

electron a particle found in atoms; an electron has a negative electric charge equal to that of a proton

energy the power to do work

fuel a material that can be burned to produce heat

gamma ray a form of energy given off by the breaking down of the nuclei of atoms

generator a device that changes mechanical energy into electricity

helium a type of atom with two protons in its nucleus

hydrogen a type of atom with one proton in its nucleus

infrared a form of energy that is invisible to human eyes but can be felt as heat

kilowatt-hour a measure of how much electrical energy is used in one hour

kinetic energy the energy that an object or particle has as a result of its motion

microwave a form of energy that can be used for communication or cooking

molecule a group of atoms that are bonded together

neutron a particle found in the nuclei of atoms; a neutron has no electric charge

nuclear energy energy that is stored in the nucleus of an atom and holds it together

nucleus (plural: nuclei) the central part of an atom, which is made of protons and neutrons

particle a tiny portion of matter

photon a tiny, weightless, invisible bundle of energy

potential energy energy that is stored in an object, molecule, or atom

proton a particle found in the nuclei of atoms; a proton has a positive electric charge equal to that of an electron

radioactive giving off energy from the breaking up of atoms

radio wave a kind of enrgy that can be used for communication

repel to push away

static electricity an imbalance of electric charges within or on the surface of a material caused by the movement of protons and electrons

tsunami a series of extremely large ocean waves caused by an earthquake or other disturbance

ultraviolet a form of energy given off by the Sun that causes human skin to darken and become damaged

vibration shaking back and forth

wavelength the distance between the peaks of a wave

work the use of a force to move an object, or the transferring of energy from one object to another

FURTHER READING

BOOKS

Electricity (Science in a Flash),
Georgia Amson-Bradshaw (Franklin Watts, 2018)

Energy (Ecographics),
Izzi Howell (Franklin Watts, 2020)

Renewable Energy (Putting the Planet First),
Nancy Dickmann (Wayland, 2019)

Where Does Lightning Come From? (A Question of Science),
Anna Claybourne (Wayland, 2020)

WEBSITES

Find out more about energy from these websites:

kids.britannica.com/kids/article/solar-energy/433607

spaceplace.nasa.gov/menu/sun/

www.bbc.co.uk/bitesize/articles/zw7q96f

www.ducksters.com/history/us_1800s/steam_engine_industrial_revolution.php

INDEX